Contents

Forward

I wrote this book to combine the answers to many of the questions that I have gotten asked over the years. It is not by any means a comprehensive practice management book, nor is it meant to be. My goal is to get the reader to think differently about their practice. This industry is always changing and what I write will soon be obsolete. This has been my frustration at times with much of the "advice" that I hear. It is often out of date or not applicable to some practices of a certain demographic. Every day you need to assess your situation and ask, "Should we still be doing it this way?"

It is up to the reader to think about their demographics and changing business climate and adjust to the situation and the times. Much of what I have learned was by being a listener. I listened to other business owners and sales representatives in the field. Nothing about the book is intended to steer you towards or away from any particular entity or product, but rather to help you figure out what is best for your office. What is your long-term goal?

What works for your situation?

In most cases, you will be the CEO, CIO, and COO of your new office. If you are very fortunate, you may

be able to hire an office manager who is well trained. But you always need to find out what their training was like and on what topics it was focused. Maybe they know a lot about one particular topic, or they are a really hard worker. The purpose of this book is to serve as a guide to your office. It is not the "end all" of books, but hopefully it will train you and your staff to think differently about operations and profit. It is meant to be different than every other book or guide on the topics. I was also not the goal to rehash everything that every other consultant is doing or saying. By all means, many of them are experts today in what they do. This book should cause you to think differently about the old ways of consulting and cause you to search out new consultants to guide you through your journey. The things in this guide should merely be talking points to continue the conversation with the consultants and representatives around you who can continue to mentor you. In this guide you will see me pointing out the things that the old consultants used to say, but this is a new day in eyecare. One of the doctors who used to work for me once said "Back in the 80s and 90s our biggest struggle was figuring out where to put the money that came in, but it's gotten a lot more complex now!"

I am not your guy for pro-forma or a practice evaluation, nor do I want to be. Sure, I muddled my way through a pro-forma and got a small business loan surprisingly after the housing market crash. I'm a nuts-and-bolts kind of guy, and you will see that in this guide. I am happy to direct you to the outstanding experts in our field who have mastered these topics beyond these nuts and bolts. My talents lie in the scrappy details of daily operations and planning. Most of my career was in everything that surrounds the exam lane but not in it. It is also not my goal to be "smarter than your staff". Your staff is in the trench of your particular situation every single day. They are the experts on the front lines of your bottom line. It is my goal only that this book helps you and them think differently, and that they in turn come up with the real genius!

A little about me:

I started my career surfacing lenses in a small independent laboratory over 22 years ago. After a few years I became an optician and then a store manager. After dispensing for a few years, I purchased my own practice from an optometrist. It was a small office that was struggling. I worked hard to turn the practice around in an extremely saturated market. Later on, I began working in wholesale and have had careers in both wholesale laboratory sales as well as wholesale frame sales. During this time, I received my bachelor's degree and master's degree in healthcare management. I then went on to become Vice President of Digital Solutions at the company I worked for. Each day I manage the development and sales of the latest digital tools for selling eyewear. I am thankful to interact with hundreds of experts around the globe who are branching out into omnichannel optical sales. Recently I was chosen to be part of the Forbes Business Development Council. I enjoy speaking at tradeshows and conventions about the latest developments affecting eye care businesses. I have a deep-rooted passion for independent practice and their continued success. What gets me really excited each day is making an impact or sharing the nuggets I have gathered from others along the way.

Cold Start or Re-start

When we walked into our own office for the first time, we were filled with aspirations of success. The problem is, we had just spent a ton of money just to walk through that door and more is needed. We want more sales and more patients, but how do we get there? Whether you are a cold start practice or recently purchased an older practice, many of your challenges are the same. As a new optician owner, I had to operate on a shoestring, and I also knew that I needed to turn a struggling practice around. Not only were there challenges, but I was now responsible for anything from the color of the new sign to what brand of toilet paper to buy! I walked around the dispensary and looked at the inventory. It was all junk. I knew that I not only needed new inventory, but I also needed to completely change the perception that had been built in the community that we were not a quality eye wear office. The challenge in a cold start or a low volume office is that you may buy a large inventory of products just to have it sit and get stale. Just because you bought a nice inventory does not mean that people will immediately flood in your doors. Even if word begins to travel that you have great product, the patients who hear about it may not be due for an exam yet. With the cycle of exams often being two to three years these days, the runway to get a solid cycle of new patients can be a long one. This is the challenge with marketing that many analysts do not understand about our industry. The target audience must get top of mind advertising when they are due for an exam specifically. Years ago, I worked for a large chain who concluded that television advertising had zero impact on sales. I would agree that short-term advertising in our industry is money in the wind unless it is a part of a large-scale, long-term model.

Digital marketing is key in our era. In the early days of my office, I had a lot of free time between patients. I constantly looked at my Google ranking on local searches to see how I matched up with the competition. There is no secret formula, and even if there was, it would be completely obsolete by the time this book was published. One day I would make it to the top of the Google rank, then the next day I might drop a spot. What I found was that Google is always changing its algorithm. It became a regular habit of mine to search for my business type and see where I ranked. Once I noticed I wasn't ranking as high as I would have liked, I examined what others were doing to rank higher. Maybe it was the content on their Google Business listing or maybe they were running some AdWords ads at the time. I would adjust and continue to keep my ranking. There are many other key factors such as reviews, backlinks, and how your page loads. In the old days a business knew that to have the best spot in the Yellowpages, they needed a name that started with "A" to be first. (I can't believe the day has come that I have to explain what the Yellowpages were, but back in the day every phone number was listed in a book that was mailed out by the phone company called a phone book, this was before the internet. In the front of the book were residential phone numbers on white pages, the back portion was all yellow paper where the businesses were listed alphabetically.) There wasn't much strategy in those days besides your name and some pretty pictures to stand out in the book. If you are in a large city, it could take years to make it to the first page of a Google search for optical related stores organically. In this case it may be well worth it to spend some money to appear in an ad on the first page.

A local SEO expert can help keep you abreast of all the changes in strategy. For the content of your page, I recommend you keep it simple. No one goes on to Amazon to read the Bio of Jeff Bezos, they are there to find what they need. I am not saying that a new doctor should not tell the community a little bit about them, but this shouldn't be the main focal point of the page. Potential patients want to know how to get an appointment, what your hours are, what insurance you accept, and how to order what they need. Each of these things should be easily seen the moment they land on your page without going through long drop-down menus.

Getting on insurance provider lists:

The optical industry is unusual because of the types of insurance plans that we often see. These plans require massive discounts on our services and products. Originally, these plans lured us to join their networks by promising us that they would send us all of the patients in their network. Eventually nearly everyone joined their networks and there was little to no advantage over any other office. In a traditional business model, the cost of these discounts is equivalent to the acquisition cost of a new customer. If the plans in your area do not provide you with any actual acquisition of new customers, then this expense may be better allocated to traditional marketing aimed at cash or self-pay patients. The cost of these discounts allows you to be listed on their provider list (a form of marketing). Each plan must be carefully considered for its benefits to the office. In the beginning, you often need cash flow. It may make sense to accept certain plans in the beginning, but not as a long-term strategy. Consultants used to talk a lot about "chair cost" when determining which plans to accept. This cost was determined by adding up all of your expenses and dividing them by the number of exams slots you had on your appointment book each day.

They advocated dropping insurance plans which were at or below your chair cost. This is a great strategy when your chair is always full, but what they failed to mention is that your chair cost is the same whether your chair is empty or full. So, if you don't have any appointments, throw the strategy of chair cost out the window. Now certainly you cannot take plans that pay you less on eyewear than your acquisition cost (and there are some odd ones out there) And also remember, some of these plans will let you be an exam only provider.

Credentialling can take a long time with some plans.

Rarely, some of them can offer you a sort of "voucher" system until you are accepted. Don't be afraid to ask what the insurance does to work with new offices. Most of the time, they will tell you that you cannot bill or see any patients until after you are fully credentialed. If you are lost in the credentialling realm, it may make sense to start with an experienced optical billing company. Not only can they often get paid for more claims in a timely manner, they are also experts at credentialling. It is much easier to add a new location to a doctor who is already credentialed with the plan as a whole. This is why it may make sense as a doctor to work in another established practice for a while to get some basic credentialling out of the way. Then when you transition to your new location, you may only have to be added to that location. Also, if you are starting a whole new entity at that location, it will have to have its own NPI and be credentialed with many plans as well. Some of this is paperwork you can start on right away before the ink is dry on a purchase. There are several types of agreements that sellers and purchasers agree to for a transition. Some of them allow in the contract for a sort of transition period for the sake of credentialling and billing in an existing practice. If you are starting completely cold, I recommend getting your entity set up and your credentialling started long before picking out paint colors. If your area is saturated with third party plans, the last thing you want to do is have a bunch of claims that you cannot get paid on when you need cash flow most. It is essential to know your demographic. Does everyone in your area work in one of several large businesses with a certain insurance plan? This may be a key plan that you need to accept in order to see these patients.

Reach out to local employers.

As a part of understanding the plans in your area, I also like to identify large employers who may not have a plan at all. Where my office was, I identified several of my safety eyewear contracts that did not have an optical plan. I created an in-house discount plan for these companies and formed a relationship with their HR department. Not only did I get on their list as a safety eyewear dispenser, but their employees would know that they could get a discount on eyewear and exams at our location. This can be a great way to find some immediate growth and create some traffic in your dispensary. Early on, while staff may have less to do, have them research local businesses.

Joining Groups and Service organizations:

I found that service organizations and local business groups were a great way to engage the community and get referrals. Many of these organizations have networking breakfasts or lunches which are a great way to not only find customers but to learn from other business leaders in your community. Membership can also help you be aware of local events to participate in. These events can be great places to do screenings and tell the community what is different about your office. Strong relationships with city officials can also help when issues arise such as parking or sidewalk maintenance. Many government offices will be more apt to listen to you when they see that you are regularly engaged in the daily operations of your district.

☐

Inventory Profit

Aside from offices with a lot of medical billing, most of the profit comes through the dispensary. Many insurance plans assume a 2.6 markup on frames and many offices have a markup of 3x the list price. At first glance, you may think "How could I not make money?". Unfortunately, margins get a lot more complicated with third party plans. There are plans that have wholesale allowances and plans that have only a retail allowance. Each requires a different strategy.

Wholesale Based Plans

I have consulted many offices that didn't realize they were actually making negative margins on many frames in their inventory. There are several popular plans which reimburse based on the wholesale list price of a frame. This means that much of your markup is sometimes irrelevant on these plans. For example: Patient Smith has a popular plan with a $50 wholesale allowance and a $130 retail allowance. Your contract with this insurance may state: "For all frames at or below the wholesale allowance, the patient does not have a co-pay, for all frames over the wholesale allowance, subtract the retail allowance from your usual and customary fee, then deduct 20%. This is the patient's copay on this frame." Let's look at the math of several frames in this situation:

Frame	Wholesale	Retail	Co-Pay	Net Profit
Choice A	$49	$149	$0	$1
Choice B	$51	$149	$15.20	$16.20

Now Choice A had only a $1 net profit on this plan, but this did not include shipping, warranties, or vendor discounts. You will be in the negative on this frame. At a 20% vendor discount, you may have $10 more net profit as long as your shipping is free and your employees work for free. Then if you offer a warranty and pay to ship the new frame in and the old frame back, this frame has become very expensive.

Choice B was just $2 more in acquisition price but had $15 more in net profit simply because it was over the wholesale amount on this plan. The reality here is that cheaper isn't always better when buying frames.

Unfortunately, the world of insurance is so bizarre that you will never learn this in business school. The reaction of many who first look at these numbers is to only buy products that are above all of the wholesale plans in their area. This is not the only strategy, however, nor is it allowed by many contracts. Often the contract states specifically that you need to have a certain percentage of inventory that is completely covered by the plan. This is where high margin value frames come into play. Discount suppliers will have certain lines of frames with a very high list price and a deep discount for these plans. Offices who understand this will often have a wall or turning rack with covered frames for these plans. These frames may have an acquisition price of less than $5 with a wholesale ranging from $39-49. This allows you to offer stylish frames with a margin that will still be covered by the plan.

Retail Based Plans

For popular plans which are retail-based and do not give a wholesale allowance, there is a strategy to follow as well which may not be apparent. You might be thinking that since the plan is retail-based your margins will be fine. Remember that most plans assume a 2.6 markup. A typical retail plan may have a retail frame allowance of $130 and a reimbursement of $50 to the office. This means that for any frame in your inventory that is marked at or under $130 you will only receive $50. This is another area where a three times markup may not serve you well. For example, a frame that you paid $42 for and marked up 3x would have a retail price of $126 and would only yield an $8 margin on this plan. If you see a lot of retail plans with an allowance of $130, then my rule would be that every frame with a retail under $150 in the store would need to be a value product from a value vendor. Frames from a value vendor may have an acquisition price ranging from $5-25 and would yield a much better margin. I would pick a quality level that you like and price them as your covered frames. With value frames, most plastic frames from $5-10 are an injection molded acetate with slightly less quality than a sheet cut acetate. Above $10 you may find some sheet-cut acetates and even some 2 year warranties with the right vendor.   While many think of value vendors as only supplying $5 frames, the right value vendor may have a lot more to offer than you realize. Many of them have spent a lot of time curating collections for the very purpose of helping you profit from these plans.

To make it simple for both retail and wholesale plans, I recommend a simple strategy. Figure out what the most common retail and wholesale allowances are in your area. Then create a hard line for both when purchasing. Make sure that every frame under a certain amount retail or wholesale is purchased at a massive discount from a value supplier. Then add these frames to one board, display, or group of trays. Only direct to these trays when someone insists upon a covered item. Because you carefully selected these frames, you know that you always have a margin. Then everything else on your standard boards, be sure that both wholesale and retail are above the allowances common for your area. This will keep your margins intact.

Some offices turn to discontinued products to increase their margins. I am not 100% against this strategy, but it must be used very carefully. There are several areas of concern. Most insurance contracts forbid the use of discontinued frames or expressly state that they must have a warranty. For children with high breakage, you could easily end up in the negative. Another area of concern is when the patient spends a lot on their lens options, and you cannot simply warrantee the frame. You could end up paying for both the frame and the lenses. This could lead to a very dissatisfied customer and a negative review. It is also not a great strategy for high volume offices typically.

Let's face it, we all love pretty frames! But offices need a solid strategy when it comes to selecting frames and vendors. Once you have a strategy for what types of price points and products to stock, you need to select which vendors to purchase them from. I like to look at products in three categories: high-margin budget product

($5-10 acquisition), unbranded product, and branded product. Each of these have a certain place in the dispensary. We have examined the high-margin, value product in this chapter. Unbranded products are often quality eyewear made from all of the same materials as branded eyewear only without the brand name. This eyewear can be a huge source of margins when properly purchased. The mistakes that I see many making with this product are either overpaying for it, or poorly positioning it. Before I knew much about insurance margins, I would buy unbranded products from the same vendors that I purchased my branded product from. With these vendors, I was never getting more than a 30% discount off of list price. The problem was that the list price was too low for my insurance plans to make a margin on this eyewear. It had all the quality of branded eyewear and often came from the very same factories. Later, I discovered that I could get similar eyewear from companies which were also my value frame partners. When I purchased from them, I was consolidating vendors, saving on shipping, and securing a much larger discount (60-80%). Often times this product is overlooked for its value and is poorly positioned in the office for this reason. The truth is that many comparable branded frames are simply overpriced in comparison. A good optician should be able to touch a frame and understand its value and durability for the materials and construction. Once chosen, it should be displayed similar to branded eyewear with a slightly lower price in most situations. Remember that this eyewear will have a much better margin for your office, and always train your staff to tell the story of its quality and origins. Let the consumer know that they are saving money by avoiding simply paying for a logo or a name. Customers want to feel good about their purchase.

Certainly, branded eyewear and luxury eyewear have a place in our dispensaries. I recommend being sensitive to your demographics when choosing this eyewear. It must be profitable, durable, and what your demographic is looking to purchase. Customers will always be asking for this brand or that, but you can only stock a limited number of frames. And most "brands" have minimum "buy-ins" that could range from 20-100 pieces. I encourage offices to think about what someone is saying when they say, "I want this brand". They are often telling you that they want to look and feel good in their glasses. They want a particular feeling, and it is the job of the optician to deliver that feeling with each encounter. I recommend choosing brands that have a story. This is a powerful tool when a customer is trying to give themselves permission to make a purchase that they will feel good about. Brands with stories are often involved with a charity or social purpose. Other brands may have a story about their recycled materials or sustainability. Once you select some brands with stories, it is important to make sure that your staff knows the story well enough to tell it.

Another thing to consider is how many vendors you will work with. More vendors equates to more shipping costs, more invoices, and more appointments with sales representatives. While too few vendors can also be a risk. If you have most of your product from a very limited number of vendors, supply chain issues could leave you in a difficult situation. You could end up with long backorders or warranties that cannot be satisfied. Very small and niche lines often have less on-hand inventory and lower fulfillment rates of orders. When selecting a vendor, it is a good idea to get a feel for how their backorder rates are. If you cannot get a straight answer from a rep, then I recommend asking some colleagues about their experience with a particular vendor.

Turn Rates

I despise this term in our industry. As someone with an MBA, I have been frustrated by its misuse and overuse. At a recent conference I kept hearing the term and I asked one of the attendees, "How many times do you want to turn a frame at zero profit to make it profitable? How many times do you have to turn a frame at a $1 profit for it to be as valuable as one turn of a frame with a $10 profit?" In the optical industry someone adopted this phrase and applied it to how many times a product sells. This is an error. In every other industry turn rate is not a single item metric. It is the ratio of your cost of goods sold divided by your average inventory. It is always a function of margin, not a rate at which a style moves. The rate at which a single style moves is not an indicator of profit. In fact, it could be an indicator of the opposite. If a frame is underpriced for its value, it may be flying off the shelf. Turn rate in business is used to determine if a business has an overall poor sales strategy or has too high of holding costs. Holding cost refers to how much money is required to store or display product. This is usually related to larger items or mass floorplan layout improvement.

Holding cost has little or no bearing in most offices. Most other industries use it to control stock levels versus individual product selection. Another consideration with what is often termed "Framed Turn rate" in our industry are niche frames. Niche frames are frames that are not mainstream as far as most sales are considered. Perhaps (due to exam cycles) you only see a gentleman who wants a double bar uni-fit bridge frame once a year. Now holding this $5-10 frame is much less expensive than sending it back and then ordering it in for this patient. Other frames with low turn rates that I consider to be "must haves" are recreational safety eyewear. Each of these scenarios are reasons, in my opinion, to ditch the errant phrase "turn rate". That doesn't mean that you should keep a line that simply never sells. If it is taking up a bunch of valuable real estate on your boards, it would exchange it or ask about a buy back program from another vendor.

Markup Strategy

We have already spent a little time examining how markup is a bit complex when it relates to insurance plans. It is tempting to mark products up high in order to have more margin on some plans and then offer a discount to your cash customers. However, it is important to note that when you bill a claim stating that your "Usual and Customary" fee for a frame is a certain amount, your contract dictates that it must indeed be your usual fee. For this reason, many offices offer a "prompt pay" discount instead of a "self-pay" discount. Since the insurance companies do not offer payment the same day in most cases, you are able to avoid any contract violations. While a three times the list price markup is pretty standard, there may also be some instances where this may not work. In some markets, it may be difficult to sell a frame with a $500 list price for more than a 2X markup. Conversely, a value frame that you acquire for $5 should be marked up to a price just below your least expansive standard products.

When first opening an office, many owners are tempted to search for vendors which offer consignment. In this situation, the vendor will ship you a bunch of frames and keep a list of the amount that they are worth. Periodically, the rep will come in and replenish your frame boards and you will owe the amount of the new frames that are shipped to you that month. Your overall balance remains the same with the company until you either decide to ship the equivalent number of frames back or pay off the balance. It gets complicated when you replace the product with different priced frames, and tracking your COGS is hard. The other problem with this model is that the company will put pressure on the rep to constantly replenish product whether you are ready for another bill or not. While at first it seems like it is leaving room in your cash flow, long term it will make your cash flow impossible to control. You will not be free to just "slow your buying down" in a month where you want some extra cash flow. I prefer to buy products up front and simply ask for billing terms. On a large order, many vendors will offer split payment terms such as 30/60/90. The result is that you are paying about the same as the consignment initially, but you will not have any surprises down the road.

Stocking Strategy

Many offices have too much back stock that they will never move. Initially they began this to lessen their shipping cost on a single frame order. My recommendation is to stock several of the products that move the quickest and keep a list of frames that have sold (either in a binder or a report in your EHR). Divide the report by vendor, so that when you do need one specific frame for a patient, you can restock with one shipping charge for the whole box of product. This is crucial on value frames. If you ship one value frame at a time, the shipping is more than the frame, and your margins are cut in half instantly.

☐

Positioning in the market

By the time many Optometrists finish their long road of study, their minds begin to turn back towards their roots. Many will seek to open a location in or near their hometown. Perhaps they feel they have a strong network that would support them, or it seems safe and secure. Often, they fail to fully do the market research before selecting a place to cold start. For example, let's say that the new OD has 300 close friends. If they are able to see 10 patients a day, and for some odd reason they all immediately needed an exam, then they would have 30 days of business. This is obviously not a viable strategy. Many businesses will do a market study before entering a market, but I don't believe it has to be that complicated for a single location. This simple analysis is good prior to both a cold start and an existing practice purchase. There are three key things to look at first:

• How booked are other offices?

• What types of insurance plans are common?

• Is the community in a phase of growth or decline?

If you call a few offices and all of them have openings the same day or same week during a normal business cycle, then this is a red flag. A good place to enter the market is where many offices are booked up two weeks or more ahead of time. Many consultants would do a lot of math to determine market saturation with very little accuracy. Calling a few offices for an appointment will tell you immediately what your market saturation is like. While you are conducting this research, also take notes of how the office is positioned in the market. Do they appear to be a boutique, a family optical, or a value outlet. This will help you later as you begin to develop your own brand and fit into the market. Many today want to position themselves as a boutique or high-end optical store without determining whether the community can support a second or third boutique. If you are set on your location, you may need to accept what type of business that there is a consumer demand for. If you are flexible on your location, then you can begin to search for locations which will support the type of business model that you have dreamed of starting. This isn't to say that you could not start as one type of business model and slowly transition into another. I think some have a false impression that they will immediately siphon off patients that fit their model, but this takes years. For the most part, exams and eyewear are not impulse purchases. While other retail models provide goods and services that we may need multiple times in a single month, the cycle for eye care is much longer. Growing a loyal patient base from scratch to 5,000 or more takes years in most cases.

Those who are called "consultants" in our industry are often previous practice owners or optometrists who feel that they had a reasonable level of success and would now like to monetize their knowledge. Many of them are indeed very smart, and I have great respect for them. But remember, so many of these voices were successful in one business model in one particular demographic or location. In my career I have visited over 500 offices in various demographics. What works well for one, may be the death of another. They all have excellent things to say and teach you, but I recommend to carefully examine the context of where they practiced. Ask them detailed questions to understand if their information is about a similar demographic and market saturation as your intended location, then apply their wisdom.

Differentiation is also a key strategy to keep in mind. As you compare the makeup of the local practices, it is often far quicker to gain a following through differentiation than through direct competition. There are two key things to keep in mind: Is there a market for what I want to offer? How different is it from what is currently offered? In a more saturated market or larger market, there may be several different options within each category of eyecare office. This can make differentiation more difficult to achieve. You may want to be a boutique or a dry-eye office, but there may already be several. In a case like this it may take more work to differentiate yourself from the market.

Next, it is good to understand the common types of optical insurance in the area. While larger markets may have a vast array of plans and members, smaller communities may be much more limited. If the community is driven by one or two main enterprises, then their plans could make up 75% of your customers. Small and midsize towns may only have a few main places of employment for those who live there. This could leave you forced to accept a plan with very poor margins for the majority of your potential customers. The types of plans in an area can also be an indicator of the health of the local economy. Take note of the largest employers in the area and ask around to learn about their optical insurance.

Lastly, you should look at the overall economic health and situation of the community. Is the community shrinking or growing? Can you do a quick internet search to see the trend of the average household income in your area? Some communities may have a lot of residents, but few businesses. These are often referred to as "bedroom" communities. While these communities look appealing, everyone leaves these communities for work and business each day. Without a major employer as an anchor, there may be little daily business conducted in these communities. Are major businesses moving in or moving out? Remember that you are about to make a very long-term commitment that cannot be easily changed. The old saying is "Location, Location, Location". This was often meant to reference physically which corner you placed your business on. This does have a factor in the success of most businesses, but slightly less for healthcare nowadays. Since healthcare is not a convenience type product or an impulse purchase, the actual physical location is less important overall than the demographic of the community. For our purposes, location is a broader term of the local climate.

Now that you have done your research and know where to fit into your community, you need to begin to develop the brand of your office. We often think of a brand in terms of the logo and color scheme. But the real brand of your office is whatever your customers are left remembering from the encounter or experience. You now have a clean slate to craft your own brand and create your own experience. Two of the most powerful brands are convenience and service. Properly married together, these two concepts will turn your customers into the most powerful brand ambassadors for your business. We all have those stops on our day of errands that we dread either because they are not convenient or because the service is terrible. There are many excellent writers and resources in our industry to help you level up your service. But I feel that convenience is often overlooked. Recent studies indicate that consumers either stay with their doctor or go online for the sake of convenience. In either case, convenience was the driving factor. Convenience encompasses many things along the patient journey from scheduling all the way to delivery of the eyewear. Convenience is a brand, and it should be one of your top brands.

Why is this "brand" so important? First of all, it is not only a market driving factor, but consumers are always willing to pay a premium for convenience! The example that I like to give at conferences is a bottled soft drink. At the grocery store the price works out to about 53 cents per bottle in a six pack for a warm drink. At the convention center gift shop, I usually pay around $4.00 for a cold bottled soft drink. But I am more than willing to pay the price for a cold soft drink compared to the alternative of walking two blocks to the grocery store to pick up a warm one in a six pack. All convenience stores charge more for the exact same products. They do not pay more for these products than anyone else, but they realize that they are offering something along with the product which is convenience. Recently I needed a new passport. The cost is $130 for a new one in 13 weeks or $195 to get one in a few days. Many segments of the business world have similar cost structures. Convenience is an addon to every sale that can increase your margins and the loyalty of your patients. I encourage offices to pretend that they have never visited their store or website before. Is it easy to find what you need and accomplish your goals in a timely manner? Remember that patients are also customers! I am not advocating that you have one price for "inconvenient service" and another for "convenient service". But I am advocating that you make convenience one of your brands that customers rave about. As you build this reputation, your prices can reflect the level of service that you provide overall.

Remember that convenience in the optical world is also about how many trips they have to make to your office. Getting it right the first time is key. Yes, there will always be those "hard fits" who don't adjust well to change. But there are many things that can mitigate this. Time spent doing it right the first time will pay dividends later in removing follow-up prescription checks. It is a good idea to have your staff neutralize their existing glasses and examine what type of lens design they have had previously. Find out in detail how they are using these glasses.

Were they "over-minused" and have been using their multifocal for distance? It may be hard for them to adjust to wearing their glasses in a normal position. I had a long-time barber who had looked over his glasses for so long that he could not rotate his neck up to use a bifocal to cut hair. The problem was that he also could no longer see well by looking over his glasses either. To solve the problem, I rotated a wide seg bifocal upside-down to the top of his frame for cutting hair. Maybe it is the part of me that wanted to be a detective as a boy, but these are some of the things I enjoy about our profession. These are the custom issues which can never be solved on a cheap website alone.

Someone recently got stern with me in a social media post for referring to patients as customers. He said "We are in healthcare". To which I said, "For far too long, healthcare has forgotten that they have customers. This is why many people dread their doctor's visits, it isn't customer friendly. They are told where to sit, how long to sit, and what they are going to pay. Our industry will lose these patients to people who treat them like customers" Being a patient means being patient, and it means waiting, expenses, and poor service. I don't think anyone wants to go to a business and be treated like they are as a patient. I cannot think of one single thing positive about being a patient except for pain killers when you need them. Most of the time you only need the pain killer for what they did to you as a patient! Often times a patient must do business with you, but a customer does not. Yes, I believe that our offices do healthcare every single day, and I do not in any means want to diminish that. But the attitude about treating everyone as a patient no longer must be mutually exclusive from treating them like a paying customer.

Perhaps part of your brand is technology or a specialty practice like dry eye or sports vision, and these are great focusses. Convenience can be added to any type of practice to increase loyalty and margins. Once you have determined your vision for your brand, you can begin to build around it. Let your concepts then shape your office design and marketing. But these are only the beginning; your chosen staff will need the brand vision as well. I have also seen many opticians develop their own brand in the community. Some are known for being the only ones who can properly adjust eyewear or figure out a problem with a progressive. This is powerful branding as well, and I encourage you to empower your opticians. I have been known for several things in various communities. One successful brand I personally had was "the guy who makes great motorcycle glasses". I kept an inventory of the latest gasketed and wrap eyewear and was great at getting a quality result with the help of my laboratory. So while we often think of brand as the view of the whole office, don't forget that a microbrand within your office can be powerful also. In big box retail, we had an expression called "store within a store". The concept was that if each individual treated what they do like a separate enterprise to rise or fall, the entire store could experience the success of multiple specialty stores and revenue streams.

Don't underestimate the worth and power of an optician who has their own microbrand. I once worked in an office where an optician was known in the whole community for being the best at adjusting glasses. In hindsight, I was as good as she was. She didn't have any trick under her sleeve that I didn't have from my vast training, but she had one thing I didn't have. She had a brand. She had been in the community for many years and her customers were very loyal to her like a hairdresser or favorite insurance agent. No matter how good I was, she was always requested over me because she had a brand that people trusted. Everything about her complimented her brand. She was nice, knowledgeable, and someone you just liked to talk to. One of the most empowering things that I experienced as an employee of another office was how the doctor treated my brand with respect. When she had a problem prescription, she would walk the patient out to me and reinforce my brand to the patient. She would say "I am going to hand you over to Mark, he is an expert at hard prescriptions and prism, he will help us make a good decision about your lenses". This was a brilliant move on her part, not just for the sake of my ego. As she did this, she instilled trust in the patient that she was now being transferred to an expert for an even more focused level of care. Often times the rush of the office makes a patient feel as though they are being dumped onto an unqualified individual to just wrap things up. It elevates the entire practice while taking a burden off of the doctor as well. I will examine this along with several other concepts in the next chapter about office narratives.

Another microbrand I have witnessed in the industry is "white-glove service". May Hwen in Nashville has had a successful business of her own special brand of white glove service to residents and VIP's in the community. She begins by scheduling a large amount of uninterrupted time to devote to these clients who rely on finding that perfect look for their image. The way that she speaks to her patients and about them is really something special to see. One of her goals is to look into the person to accentuate what is beautiful about them beyond the exterior. I have also known optometrists who had VIP hours early in the morning for busy executives on Fridays. The staff enjoyed leaving work early on a Friday, and the office found that they did some of their most profitable business during these hours. Remember that "when you are available" can be a key differentiator in the market as well. In the early days of networking in my community, I spoke with a new dermatologist at a networking breakfast. He explained that his business was exploding due to one key factor: he was available. He always answered the phone and found a way to see new customers.

Within months he had his own clientele.

Office Narratives

As exciting as a new office or new position may be, there are days that work is just work. On these days there is no magic dust, and we struggle just to accomplish our tasks and get to the next thing. Some days the staff may feel this way while the exam lane is immune to it and vice versa. In these moments we are tempted to create bad habits and bad narratives. We begin to see every patient as "more work". This mindset is where service utterly implodes. And while the office owner may potentially make more money from a busy day, many staff members will not. Great business owners understand how to incentivize their staff both financially and emotionally for when the going gets tough. No customer should ever be treated like a new inconvenience; however, it is often written on the face of office staff from the moment a customer walks through the door. Again, no one wants to be treated like a problem.

During these busy or stressful times, we often adopt narratives or sayings which take away from the experience and decrease sales. I will begin with a list of common phrases and alternatives for a better experience:

Bad	Better
How many boxes of contacts do you want?	A year supply will save you this much money
Do you know what insurance you have?	Can I help you find your insurance plan?
We will see you on Tuesday	We look forward to seeing you, please bring your prescription sunglasses as well to the visit.
These are not under warranty	Let me call the manufacturer to see if there is a slight chance that these still have a warranty, I will try to get you an excellent discount
No, your glasses are still not here yet, we will call you when we do get them	We sent your glasses to a custom lab, let me reach out to them for a status to see if I can move them through the production
If you bring them in, we will see what we can do	If you text the office a picture of where they are broken or apart, we will get right back with you about your options

Do you want what is covered by your insurance	Let's figure out what style you like then see what your insurance will contribute. Its different for each frame and we have a lot of styles in different price points. Once we know your style, then we can narrow the selection down further.
Those look good	That frame really compliments your color palette as well as your natural face shape
No problem	My pleasure
You probably just need to adjust to them	There are quite a few different things that make up your prescription. I want to be sure that we check each one of them so this goes as smoothly as possible for you with the fewest trips. I am going to ask you a series of questions about your vision to try to figure out exactly which part of the prescription or lens needs adjustment.

How many boxes of contacts do you want?

We all fall into this habit at times, and the answer is usually "one or two". It is a good practice to have a chart of the rebates for an annual supply and an inoffice discount. Often when combined with the insurance allowance, the patient is saving a lot of money by purchasing a one year supply up front. We would also prepare the envelope and print the receipt for them to get their rebate from the manufacturer. This phrase should be replaced in every practice.

Do you know what insurance you have?

So many times, the answer to this question is "no". Optical insurances are notorious for not giving any documentation to their customers. Instead of being angry and showing obvious disgust at the very beginning of the transaction, just accept this as part of the gig. All staff should be trained not to let negative emotions show to the customer. I learned this when I used to work with a funeral director as a young preacher. He said to me "Mark, I am always in a hurry to the next thing on the inside, but I never let it show on the outside. These people are going through a lot". And we also never know what our patients may be going through in their lives. It is important to be present in every moment of our lives both at work and at home.

We will see you on Tuesday.

Now there is nothing inherently wrong with this statement, but there isn't anything great about it either. It represents one of many missed opportunities in our business to be great instead of okay. Now I took this idea from a class I had almost 20 years ago at an educational. The keynote speaker encouraged everyone to say at the reception desk "Please bring your prescription sunglasses to your appointment". The main idea was that those who didn't have any would wonder "Does everyone have prescription sunglasses? Should I have some?" From the moment of first contact they were now a subtly operating sales machine. From the moment of first contact, this consumer is being given the mental permission to make a purchase. This is a powerful mindset to incorporate all the way through the customer journey. You have also simultaneously tapped into FOMO or the "Fear of missing out".

These are not under warranty.

Again, this isn't a terrible phrase, but it is often said for terrible reasons. Many times, the motive of the person saying it is to just quickly rid themselves of the most recent problem that walked in the door. Every person who walks in is an opportunity to sell convenience, even a warranty. The main goal here is to appear to be their advocate and not their mortal enemy. They are used to being told no, and in fact they expect it. Likely, the previous day and the car ride to the store they have played over in their minds what they will say when you say "no". Even if you eventually have to tell them no, disarm them immediately by moving over to their side of the situation.

No, your glasses are not here yet.

The average office will say this several times each day. If your laboratory offers a WIP or "work in progress report" this is a great resource. Take a slight second to reinforce to the patient that their lenses are custom made each time. The average person knows very little about the process and it is often very mysterious to them. We forget how uneasy they may be that they just spent a lot of money, to wait an undisclosed amount of time, hoping that they can see and look good. All of this uncertainty has them uneasy. Emphasize that you want to deliver the best product possible the very first time.

If you bring them in, we will see what we can do.

I am not sure why in this century we are still having customers drive to the office with broken glasses, then make them drive back again to pick them up after we order them. If the office has a dedicated text line, you could simply have them text a picture of the broken part to determine if it simply needs a quick repair or if you need to order a replacement. Saving this time will greatly increase their attitude in this difficult situation. Let them know that you would like to save them a trip. It also saves the resources of your busy dispensary.

Do you want what is covered by your insurance?

This is another one to make completely taboo in your office. The motive behind this question is to try to hurry along with the sale. The inevitable answer to this question is "Yes, I would like what is covered". The truth is we rarely like or want what is covered. We want to feel good and look good. If the customer asks the question first, then reply with "It varies by frame manufacturer, first let's try to figure out what your style is, then maybe I can find similar ones at multiple coverage levels."

Those look good.

This is an attempt to close a sale by reinforcing the decision of the patient. This in itself is the beginning of a good close, but not a great one. Take the time to be personal and really build confidence in the person about themselves and the purchase. I have often witnessed both a struggle with self-confidence and the struggle to give themselves permission to purchase. I like to reinforce that their glasses match their palette or shape well. I want to create excitement about returning to pick up their new eyewear. They want to feel like a new person regardless of their budget. They will remember the way you made them feel above every other part of the transaction.

No problem.

This one had been written about often but is worth a reminder. "No problem" sounds like the person may have actually been a problem, but you are doing them a huge favor by dealing with it. Instead, people would rather feel like they are a pleasure to you.

You probably need to adjust to them.

While we all know that this statement is often very true, no one wants to hear it. I was always the go-toguy to figure out difficult prescriptions and I enjoyed it at times. One day I realized that a patient was exaggerating and even lying about their symptoms despite the fact that I was doing everything I could to help them. I could tell from their prescription change that there was no way they were experiencing what they said. I even used a couple of acuity tests to confirm that they were actually seeing better in the new glasses. At this point I became less interested in what was causing their discomfort as I was in figuring out what I was doing wrong. I realized that they were exaggerating because they didn't think I really wanted to help them. I was giving them all of my attention and asking dozens of questions trying to diagnose the exact issue. But it suddenly occurred to me that they had been through something similar before. They had heard the same questions before, but the whole transaction ended with "You need to adjust to them". I had no intentions of telling them that, but I also had not taken any particular steps to reassure them that I really actually wanted to find something in the glasses that I could definitively change to make them happier. I realized that this was my fault in communicating my motives effectively. I stopped the diagnostic process for a moment to explain the fact that there are so many parts of a prescription which seem almost invisible to the naked eye, that I wanted to be sure to change the correct one the very first time. I then explained that I had a series of questions and tests to do with them to help me in this process of figuring out what to change. Like magic, the entire tone of the encounter changed, and I learned a great deal about myself and humans.

This is not by any means an exhaustive list. But I encourage you to listen to your staff and yourself as you engage with customers. Realize that they are a patient and a customer. Make a habit of listening to the tones of your office. The goal is not to micromanage or to work harder. The goal is to be more profitable and work less. These steps are not necessarily harder physically, but they may be harder mentally at first. Once these things are engrained into the office narrative, things will actually be much smoother. It can be fun as well. Come up with creative ideas to incentivize a positive narrative. One idea is to fill a jar with dollar bills and remove a dollar each time someone says a taboo phrase. Incorporate fun and laughter into the transition period of the office narrative. Then at the end of the month, what is left in the jar is used for an office lunch or party.

Office culture doesn't just happen without intention, but it needs to be real and not a slogan on a sign. What you bring into the office is a large part of what you will get out. If you bring stress and negativity, you will have staff that is stressed and negative. Recognize what motivates each staff member. Some are motivated financially, while others are motivated by encouraging words or empowering speech. Many staff members just want to be respected and to be part of the process. When I purchased my office, I included the staff when we purchased product. I asked them what they wanted to sell. Immediately he sales went up considerably. The staff was excited about what they were selling for the first time. But every person has their own motivating factors in their career. What may work for one, may be the opposite for another. Begin exploring this from the moment you begin to interview a prospective employee by asking "What motivates you at your job?" I have been asked this many times as a "cookie-cutter" question at an interview, and it is easy for most to perceive if it is sincere or a formality.

Working with your Laboratories

By far the biggest bill you will pay each month is the laboratory bill. It is very important to make sure that your laboratory is aligned with your goals for both the immediate and long-term purpose. I cannot stress enough to love your labs and build a great relationship with them! Perhaps the bill is so painful that we close our eyes to everything surrounding it. Many laboratories today are owned by the very competition you face down the road. No matter how attractive their prices may be, this may be inconsistent with your long-term strategy of independence. If you have to accept a lot of thirdparty plans, you may be forced to use a laboratory associated with a chain of retail stores for a portion of your work. Your laboratory rep can be one of your greatest training resources for new products in the marketplace.

For your non-insurance work, you are free to use whichever lab you feel comfortable with. Many offices do not understand that they have power to negotiate with their lab. These labs understand that it is very difficult to acquire a new customer, and they are more willing to negotiate than your frame vendors may be able to. I had a certain insurance plan which had a very low lined bifocal reimbursement rate. I explained this to one of the laboratory representatives and they created special pricing on this one category of lens for me.

There are many other benefits that your lab can often provide you with. Many of them have accounts and programs with frame vendors. This can be beneficial in multiple ways. They may offer a frame and lens package which can increase your margins. Another benefit of a lab which stocks frames is that you may be able to save on shipping for the occasional single frame order. Often times shipping costs are overlooked by an office in their daily operations. These can add up quickly, and it is best to consolidate shipments wherever possible. I have had numerous accounts that ship one frame at a time each day, and often the same frame. On a value frame, you have instantly cut your margin in half with shipping. Some companies also have a handling fee for only one frame. Often times a $5 frame just became a $13 frame after shipping and fees. I always advise stocking deeper in styles that you know move quickly and place less frequent orders.

Laboratories are also excellent resources for inhouse finishing supplies such as stock lenses and blocking pads. In-house finishing is a great resource and does not have to be as intimidating as it sounds. Today's modern equipment is often very userfriendly. For your self-pay customers or insurance plans without a contract lab, you can really increase your margin and level of service. If you assume that a laboratory may charge you $50-80 for a pair of single vision lenses with an anti-reflective coating, you can save a lot of money by using a stock lens purchased for $8-12 a pair. Even in a low volume office, the savings can quickly surpass the monthly payment on a refurbished edger. For my office, the edger was also part of a larger business growth strategy. I kept a small number of stock lenses on hand for certain situations. In my town there was an ophthalmologist who did cataract surgery follow-ups on Wednesdays. He would send his patients to me to remove one lens and edge in a plano lens until their surgery on the other eye. I would purchase plano (non-prescription lenses) in bulk for 20 cents each. I told each of the patients that if they returned for their replacement pair, the lens fee would be subtracted from their final purchase. These customers appreciated this service and eventually became eyewear customers.

The other benefit of having an edger on site was the ability to get an excellent fit when a patient wants to keep their existing frame. If an office needs to rush an order, they can also order an uncut lens from their laboratory to speed up delivery time. For plus powered lenses, it is important however to include as many accurate measurements of the frame as possible including ED, B, DBL, and A measurements. This allows the laboratory software to surface the lens as thin as possible while still allowing the lens to cut out properly in the edger.

I encourage an office to experiment with stock lenses and get comfortable edging all types of material and coating combinations. The more types of lens upgrades that you are comfortable with edging, the higher your margins will be. There are great margins to be had on single vision coated lenses in materials like mid and high index. Whenever I was testing a new edger or training a new staff member, I would ask the laboratory to send me a variety of uncut lenses that did not pass inspection. These are a great way to hone your skills without sacrificing stock lens inventory. When I was a laboratory representative, I would also train new staff members on equipment at my accounts as a service to them. Your laboratory wants you to succeed as much or more than any of your vendors. There are many ancillary benefits to creating a strong relationship with them as we have already seen.

As you begin to refine the daily process of your office and select the software products that make your daily tasks easier, you may want to discuss this with your lab representative as well. Before you are heavily invested in an Electronic Health Record system or Practice Management System, you may want to consult with your lab to see which ones will interface with their electronic order system. Transmitting an electronic order can reduce several points of data entry error and speed up the turnaround time of your orders. There are many offices that still use paper or even handwritten orders. When an order like this is received at the laboratory, it is up to the data entry department to accurately interpret what is ordered without missing anything. When you utilize digital ordering, you can rest assured that the system will not lose any of your data.

Another under-utilized facet of a laboratory is its access to white label products. These are lenses and coatings sold without the expense of a brand name. Over 20 years ago I was sitting in the break room of the optical laboratory where I worked reading a technology magazine. The magazine explained that high end watch companies were creating their watch faces with "free form" generators. This technology had not hit our industry in the mainstream just yet. At the time, a handful of "freeform" lenses were being surfaced overseas and imported under one of the brand names. I commented to my boss, "as soon as these machines get a little cheaper, any guy with a cad background can analyze a progressive and have their own as good or better than what we are making today". I didn't know how correct I was. Not many years after that, I began to see freeform generators installed not only into laboratories in the US, but directly into offices. Now every laboratory has the freedom to have their own progressive line. Without all of the marketing fees of the big named lens companies, these labs are able to offer the latest innovations for a fraction of the cost. This is a big win for the office as well as the patient. I encourage you to explore the white label lens options available at your laboratory for your patients.

In addition to the latest in lens design, they are also often able to offer the latest in coating design at a fraction of the price as well. Many of these coatings are made on the exact same machines with the exact same chemicals as a coating with a brand name. I encourage you to order some for yourself and test out the quality for your self-pay customers and insurances which allow you to select your own products and suppliers.

Another overlooked benefit your laboratory may offer is a discount on second pairs. When this discount is combined with the white label options we discussed, the result can be a much lower laboratory bill. I encourage every office to have standard second pair discount for their self-pay customers or insurances without a network lab. Many laboratories will offer up to 50% off of the list lens price on a second pair (it is not typically in addition to any other price discounts). In turn, you may consider a 30% off promotion for these customers to increase the chance of a second pair sale. We always positioned it like this "Mr. Smith, we have a second pair discount of 30%, but since we also do not have to use certain brands on an insurance plan, I can also

get the cost down even further with some in-house branded lenses. When it is all said and done, your second pair won't cost you more than your co-pays on your insurance pair" This is an excellent way to position a second pair. Figure out a plan that works with your laboratory and their offerings to increase your second pair sales.

I would also use a unique strategy to sell a pair of glasses to an individual who purchased an annual supply of contact lenses. Whenever someone asked, "Should I use my insurance for my glasses or my contacts?" I would tell them that with their plan, "I can bill your contacts to the insurance which takes away your glasses lens benefit for the year, but since you are getting an annual supply on your contacts, I can still bill a frame to your insurance. I will bill the frame and then give you 30% off of your lenses. Then, on top of the 30% off, I am able to use inhouse branded lenses in your glasses to save even more. So, in effect, your glasses won't cost you more than they would have if we billed your insurance. But now you are getting both, and I am going to get you a rebate from the contact lens supplier for your annual supply." These customers were ecstatic with this explanation. I would write out all of the math on their insurance claim authorization form for them to see the savings. This strategy worked over and over again with certain plans.

It is important to note that this strategy only works with certain insurance plans, and the customer has to have an annual frame allowance available to use. Some plans only offer frames every other year to the patient. Before each day, we would have our staff print off what each patient was eligible for before their appointment so we could instruct them. Also remember that the rules are always changing, but my goal is to teach you strategies that you can adapt to any situation.

☐

EHR and Practice Management Systems

These systems can be expensive and often have large annual maintenance fees on top of their lease price. Some may be tempted to "cheap out" when it comes to this software, but there are several key considerations. From the perspective of a long-time practice manager, I like to know that the software will interface with the key systems that I have, have a vast recall system, and make daily operations simple. Everything else to me is just fluff. As a movie fan and business major, "Show me the money!!" I want to know exactly how it will make me more money.

Recalls and messaging systems are some of the key ways that the system can create new revenue. When selecting one for my office I went to a number of trade shows and spoke with their representatives about how customizable the recall system was. Most of them could not answer any of my recall questions and commented that "no one asks that". I was appalled, what do you want other than highly efficient marketing set to auto mode? Yes, I want a great UI/UX, easy drop-down menus, and simplified patient check out options. But first and foremost, I want this expensive software to make money. Successful practice recalls involve not only one communication when an exam is due, but multiple follow-up communications in place when an appointment has not been scheduled. With multiple follow-ups I was able to greatly improve my yearly exam compliance rate with patients. I also wanted to be able to do targeted marketing efforts to various segments of patients by insurance type or demographic. A robust recall system is needed for these efforts and well worth the price tag. "Cheaping out" on an EHR can be a dangerous mistake for many reasons. Another item to consider is how well the system will integrate with other systems.

As you begin to set up a new office or remodel an existing one, it is a good idea to speak to your equipment provider before making a final decision on your software. Digital phoropters, retinal cameras, and autorefractors can all seamlessly transmit their results to the software to save you time and entry errors. Once a prescription has been created on the phoropter, it can be transmitted to the software and ultimately to the very surfacing machine at your laboratory without a single human intervention or error. Compatibility with each of these systems should be considered if an upgrade or new equipment is an option.

The next main area where an EHR can affect revenue is the billing of claims. Optical claims billing is often more difficult than some medical claims alone. While most medical insurance companies generally play by an accepted group of rules, Optical insurance companies often work by their own rules and make up their own special codes. If you hire an experienced medical biller, they will have to get up to speed on a lot of the nuances to optical billing. Then if you decide to bill both medical and optical on the same procedure, things get even more tricky. In the beginning, the revenue that a billing company can save you may well be worth their fees. Over time you will learn from them what diagnosis codes can go with what types of procedures. Fortunately, many of optical plans have their own "simplified" billing portals for optical claims. Even though these types of plans are restrictive, they are often easier to bill once you get the hang of it. But for many HMOs, state programs, and health plans, you will rely heavily on the billing software embedded into your EHR. Because of this, the data entered into the program about the patient's name, address, and guardians must match their insurance card exactly or the claims will be denied. Many health insurance companies are in a constant (unfair and borderline fraudulent) search for any unmatched field in the claim (no matter how small) to deny the claim. A claim could be denied because you spelled the street name of the child's parent wrong, but it was correct everywhere else. Not only do you have to load accurate information into the software for each patient, but you also need to set up several other fields. You will need to accurately set up the doctors' information into the software with all of his provider numbers and NPI. You will also need to set up each insurance into the software that you plan to bill (whether electronically or otherwise). The software will also likely require a subscription to a clearinghouse or electronic gateway to transmit the claims. Each clearinghouse will have specific data that will have to be added to the software for each insurance as well.

Clean data is a must from end to end in your system. There are over 30 fields on a claim that I believe are only designed to give them another reason to deny the claim. You will find that their rejections are often vague and misleading. From the time that you submit a claim, the clock ticks on that claim. You may not even receive your rejection on a claim until it is almost too late to refile.

You will hear a lot of consultants in big cities say "Just don't take any insurance" or "I will help you stop taking insurance". While this may work in some demographics, it won't work in many. Not everyone can afford not to use their benefits, and there may not be an abundance of other types of customers. Many doctors say it with pride "I don't take insurance", and I am glad that their demographic allowed that. Just remember that it isn't a strategy that works everywhere.

On a large claim or a larger problem with medical insurance, I learned a trick from my dad that worked in my favor a number of times. At some point you may get unfairly treated by an insurance company and feel trapped by them. My father was in the insurance business for over 35 years and explained that every insurance company has to petition the Insurance Commissioner of each state that they do business in for their license on a regular basis. When I felt I was being treated unethically by an insurance company, I would fill out an online complaint form with my state insurance commissioner. At times I was shocked to immediately receive a phone call from an executive level employee at the insurance company explaining that my claim would be paid within a few days.

Insurance is a game, and the insurance company only makes money by not paying claims. Optical insurances are slightly different from health insurances because they understand that most of their customers will in fact have a claim or they would not have subscribed. Optical insurances often design plans around products that favor the items most profitable to them. They have often worked out deals to decrease their cost on certain popular lens or coating products in order to reduce their expenses. On the lens side of things, it is valuable to study your claims remittance and compare it with the copays paid by the patient. When the insurance company has a network or contract lab that they require for lenses, it becomes tricky to understand where your margins are. Many forget that though these plans seem to not pay very much, you also don't have to worry about a lab bill. Below are some generic numbers to help you understand how these plans work. A chargeback is a portion of the copay that is deducted from your claim to pay for the addons or premium options selected. Since human nature is to pick the "midgrade" item in most cases, your profit is often less in that category.

Option	Co-Pay	Chargeback	Profit
Basic Coating $40	$25	$15	
Midgrade Coating $50	$40	$10	
Premium Coating $60	$43	$17	

The chargeback will be deducted from the total amount of the claim due to you to pay for the lab services. See below.

Exam	Dispense fee	Frame Whsl	Chargeback	Total
$55	$25		$50	-$80
$50				

Exam co-pay	Frame Co-pay	Lens Co-pay	Total
$5	$46	$140	$191

Total Revenue $241

So, while the check seemed small, the total revenue was $241 and you don't have an additional lab bill to pay at the end of the month for this patient. Yes, there is a loss of control over much of your margin with plans like this, but there is also freedom from a lab bill at the end of the month. The only way to control your lens profit on plans like this is to carefully select which lens options that you offer the most. Sometimes the mid-priced ones have the lowest margin.

This is why I spend the most time discussing frame inventory profit. Selecting the right frames is the largest area where better choices can affect your margin on a plan like this.

All of these items you will be tracking and entering into your software. Good software should have excellent reporting capabilities to allow you to understand the areas of your practice that need improvement. At some point, you will have to decide how much time you want your staff to spend entering things into the software. A really good software should eliminate unnecessary steps and redundancies. But nearly every software has a weakness, and sometimes you just need to be able to move a patient through the process. With many software systems I found myself entering the order information after the patient left so that I could help another patient.

While many offices pride themselves on being 100% paperless, they also often have long service times and a patient or two getting bored while the optician is typing all of the information into the system. For this reason, my office adopted a hybrid system of paper and electronic records. Occasionally I would have to hire some office help to fill in when I was out of town. These were often retired opticians, and they would always comment, "I have never seen an office run so quickly and smoothly." Our hybrid system was designed to be quick and efficient for everyone involved. The main point is to adopt a system intentionally for your own situation and refine it. Listen to the needs of the staff and make meaningful adjustments. Most of the so-called paperless offices ordered as much paper each week as others. The only difference was that they didn't have a "chart room" full of folders and records.

Regardless of which software you decide upon, you will have to do some additional work to be sure that all of your products and prices can easily be selected. Perhaps you have worked out a deal on a particular white label product with your laboratory, but is it in your software? If your software does not make it easily selected, then staff will be less likely to offer this product. These systems are great, but they are also a big drain on staff time when trying to complete an order and move to the next patient. Even the best EHR, will need the optician to enter the amounts that the insurance is paying, the amount of the insurance discount for each item (frame, lens, options, exam, testing) before completing the checkout process. There is nothing more frustrating during checkout than to not be able to find the products in the system to begin with. Since every insurance plan is different, and every markdown and chargeback are different, this is often a stressful process. In fact, I find it harder to train this portion of the dispensary than any other piece. Some offices may accept 10 different insurances with 2 or 3 different plans under each one. Each time a new service or product is added, be sure that it is simple to address in the EHR at checkout.

Digital Marketing

Believe it or not, some will find out about this book on social media, purchase the e-book online and then scoff at the ideas in this chapter! There are offices who order their supplies online and hire employees online, but they treat the internet like a dirty word. Our world is changing quickly, and we especially cannot resist changes that are consumer driven. About every decade an industry change has everyone terrified. I can remember when everyone believed that refractive surgery was going to eliminate optometry, but it has settled into its own place in the market. Refractive surgery had limitations which largely restricted its consumer base. There are different types of limitations which restrict some consumers from purchasing eyewear online as well. But because of those who are able to order online, this market has grown by leaps and bounds.

There is no question to me that a large percentage of sales for eyewear will be online in the future, and I believe that the independent office can be a part of that market. I often compare the optical store to that of the shoe cobbler. I wasn't really alive yet when most of the hometown shoe stores closed, and I have always gotten shoes from a discount retailer. But I imagine that when the big discount shoe stores opened up that all of the cobblers said "Those shoes will never fit right. They don't even have anyone to fit them. Those shoes will never hold up. I can't believe they just let everyone measure themselves!" Soon there were only a few remaining who knew the craft. The trend was driven by the consumer who said, "I would rather have five pairs of cheap shoes each year than just one pair that I can have repaired for years". It was a trend driven by price, convenience, and fashion. People wanted to be able to change their look more often, and they were okay with shoes that didn't last as long. Investors saw a huge untapped potential that the cobblers refused to consider. Investors could find more revenue by selling many more pairs for less than a single pair at a high price. Many eyewear shoppers are seeking some of the same goals with their eyewear. While we like to consider glasses to be a medical device, to many consumers it has more to do with fashion and expression. The consumer is driving the change in the market and demanding variety. In this chapter we will discuss all forms of digital marketing and ecommerce along with the consumer expectations.

When I first became a sales rep, offices were just beginning to understand that they needed a website and a Google listing to be found by customers. I can remember the day when my secretary threw away the phonebook as soon as it was delivered. I was appalled and said, "Why did you do that?" to which she responded, "When was the last time that you used one?" The thought that my habits had completely changed because of the internet had never occurred to me until that moment. I knew that I needed to help my wholesale customers get online quickly. Not long after that, I added contact lenses to my website for sale. Since contact lenses have been commoditized by the market, a large number of offices have added contact lenses to their own site. When properly implemented, it can save phone calls to the office and time by the staff to ship them to the patient. Some companies charge a fee for their fulfillment services, but there are ways to get direct fulfillment set up without a fee. A custom website can ensure that your fees all come directly to the practice without a middleman. Some sites even offer automated replenishment reminders which can increase sales as well as lens wearing schedule compliance. Despite the acceptance of online contact lens sales, a large number of offices remain opposed to online eyewear sales. Regardless of what products you list on your site, there are some hurdles to overcome first.

One of the problems facing a practice with any type of product on their site is that no one knows they have products for sale there. You are not Amazon, and no one knows to look on your site for products. There are only two ways that you can be readily seen by potential customers: organically or through marketing. To be found organically means that your website and traffic are already so good, that when someone searches for "contacts" or "glasses" you show up on the first page near the top. This is nearly impossible for a company outside of the fortune 500 players. Everyone else who appears on the first page pays to be there by keyword and region. My point is, just by making a site, you will not have sales. You need a strategy for selling either contacts or glasses online. There are many "free" strategies that you can use to let customers know that you have contacts or glasses available for purchase online. The first strategy is to use all of your current means of communication to let your existing customers know that this is an option for them. I encourage offices to add a QR code linking to their site to everything that they have printed, especially their prescription forms. Anyone who leaves with a copy of their prescription without making a purchase should have information in hand about your website and a brief call-to-action encouraging them to do so. All of your outbound texts and emails to patients should include some sort of marketing to plant seeds for a potential sale. Every single time you communicate with a patient, there should be some messaging included either about your products, services, or website. This growth is exponential, because Google looks at the traffic on your site when figuring out how to rank it on a page. The more traffic you get, the more traffic you will get. But now that you may have figured out how to get them to your site, what will they find?

Many times, when you look up an optometrist or a dentist, you find lengthy staff bios and blogs about conditions that you may not have. I recently heard a DJ on the radio say that the dentist's FAQ section never has anything that is frequently asked. She was disappointed that she couldn't readily know if her insurance was accepted, how much certain types of procedures were, or if certain procedures were painful. The very first page of your site should have everything that someone would immediately need from how to schedule to immediate product links and insurances accepted. Often, I will visit a site and find that they do sell some products, but I have to go through several tiers of a menu system to even find a link to them. I encourage practice owners and managers to visit their favorite websites and examine all of the elements that they see first, second, and third.

When someone visits your site, can they immediately click on what they might need without searching? A good website manager can use analytics to tell you exactly what pages were opened, and how long someone stayed on each page.

With your website built, there is still more work to do. Google and review sites allow you free listings for local searches. A local search is when some searches "Eye Doctor near me" or "Eye Doctor in my town". This is a free organic listing that is much easier to compete with than a general search someone may do for "Eye Doctor" all over the world. Depending on how many practices are in an area, it may not be difficult to rank among them in a Google business listing. This is called "Local SEO". You can either claim your own free listing or have your web developer do it for you. You are able to add images, a link to your website, and hours here. The more information that you provide, the better that you will rank in a local search. This is also a changing algorithm, so it is good practice to regularly search common terms to see how you rank. Remember that more people will search terms like "Eye Doctor" than those that will search for "Optometrist". Perhaps it is the dumbing down of society over time, but the simplest key words perform better. I am always appalled by the billboards on the side of the road that say "Big Truck Wreck? Call us for help." They learned in marketing to dumb down key words, but they didn't realize that this was for hidden keywords. When there is a picture on the billboard of a tractor trailer in an accident, even the illiterate should get the point. In summary, keep your keywords simple, but keep your advertising more formal. Each of these keywords can be set up in your

Google Business preferences and embedded in your website. Again, your local SEO expert can help with this.

Listing Frames on your site

I have had many consultations with offices that are interested in showing frames on their site, but many of them have misconceptions about this. Typically, they will tell me that they want to show every frame that they have in their store on their site. I usually ask them how often they refresh their selection, if they know what is in stock with their vendor, and if they have photos of all of these. After I have asked a few of these questions, they begin to understand that this is a nearly impossible logistical task today. I then ask them what their goals are for listing frames. In my opinion there are only two reasons to actually show a frame on your website: To let people figure out what they want to wear or to actually sell them a pair. But there is an assumption by many that if they see beautiful glasses on their site, they will schedule an appointment and become a new customer. Unfortunately, there is not much data that this is what the consumer is actually looking for online or is the motive for visiting a particular location. Several recent studies suggest that customers who plan on getting an exam locally will visit between two and three websites first to figure out what shapes and colors that they like. Those who visit a site, however, with the motive purchase eyewear are often seeking an inexpensive pair.

I am not saying that there is no value in listing what brands you carry in case someone happens to be looking for a certain brand, but physically showing each frame may not yield any benefits for the amount of work involved. Based on the data that I see, patients need two things from a frame site: Lowcost products and a variety of styles. Tools like virtual try-on can really help you capture the customers who are on your site. You have spent a lot of money on advertising to get them there, and virtual try-on is a sort of insurance policy to convert them. It will not necessarily bring new people to your site unless you are specifically advertising this feature. Remember that your customer base has no idea what you have on your site unless you give them a reason to visit it. I recommend that if you are going to list frames on your site, then you should be advertising it actively to your customer base each day. One way to do this is to add a link to your site in your recall messages and appointment reminders. Much of your success will be from the little things that you add to what you are already doing. It isn't about doing more; it is about doing differently. If customers are already going to other sites to view eyewear, then they know that they will not find those products in your store. They are simply wanting to try-on some frames before their visit. Part of this may be due to time constraints, but others may just be lost in the array of endless possibilities of fashion. But the last thing you need is them being lured in by another site because you don't have the option on your site. Encourage your customers to visit your site before their visit to try-on glasses instead of your online competition. If they do not make a purchase the same day, follow-up with messaging that encourages them to visit your online offering.

When you consider a virtual try-on, another thing to consider is the cost of digital assets. Currently the cost of getting a quality 3D image of a frame far exceeds the cost of the frame itself. And even though thousands of frames are being scanned and modeled each month, it is still impossible to keep up with the arrival of new products. Even if the scanners could keep up with your changing inventory, someone would have to add both the 2D frame image and the 3D image to your website. In the future, machine learning algorithms will likely make this much more streamlined. Until then, it is important to understand the goals of the patient as well as your own goals for your website. The patient is seeking a variety of "looks" to try on. Focus on getting a variety of "looks" verses a variety of brands. You can always use some real estate on your page to let them know what your latest brands are, and it is a good idea to have staff engage your social media pages wearing them. For those wishing to sell eyewear online, consider the motives of the online shopper as opposed to the "online browser". They are often a parent looking for a cheap pair to replace what their child broke, or a man looking for a pair to be rough with during outdoor activities. Understanding the buying profile of the online shopper is key. Most online sales today are under $100 and consist of a value frame with a single-vision lens. When you consider a virtual try-on as part of this equation, the asset cost could destroy your margins. I encourage potential sellers to choose value products which are already available in a virtual try-on. Imagine choosing a vendor for this product to save $1.00 per frame in acquisition cost, only to turn around and pay $200 per style to have 3D images created for your virtual try-on. When considering your margins online, there are vastly different factors to consider compared to your costs associated with an in-person sale. Many of the costs related to product handling can be eliminated with an ecommerce site integrated with automatic fulfillment of products. On top of this, these sales can happen 24 hours a day while the lights are off and the doors are locked. The goal should not be to convert in-store customers into online customers, but the goal should be to re-capture any revenue that was headed online regardless. Capture rate is defined as the number of patients who have an exam who ultimately purchase eyewear from you. All of the consultants will reference this number, and longtime office owners will brag about their numbers. But like any number, they can be deceiving. The traditional way of tracking capture rate cannot estimate how many customers ultimately purchased a second pair online as a back-up pair or hobby pair. Capture rates as a whole are shrinking, but I propose that there are more missed opportunities than the numbers reflect.

There is no magic formula for success. If there was one, tomorrow it would be different. Algorithms change, and economic situations change. As Ross on the iconic show Friends would say, "Pivot!!" By the time this book hits the shelf, the latest marketing tools may once again have taken a drastic turn. When I entered the industry over 20 years ago, I could not have imagined the changes that have come. I certainly don't know what is around the corner for our industry, but there are some things that never change. There are innovative and dynamic personalities are found in pockets of success in every corner of our industry. These people find the small changes that can impact the success of their business. They write their own office narratives and control the culture inside it. They are responsive to the market and remain nimble. I encourage you to be selective about the voices you listen to, but by all means, find some who have gone down your path!

Measuring Success

Goals that cannot be measured are unlikely to be obtained. Utilizing practice management software is the first key step to measuring your success. Most PMS systems offer some limited practice metrics. But to really dive deep into the metrics of your practice, many offices use KPI software. This software is able to extract data from your PMS system and organize it for better comparisons and reports. These reports aggregate data and synthesize it for simple viewing. This type of software is also able to be very granular in the level of filtering and reporting the data. Not only can the KPI (key performance indicators) dashboard give you valuable insights into the revenue growth trends of the practice, it can often display the data by staff, insurance plan, and provider.

Making data-driven decisions removes emotion and subjectivity from your business decisions. For example, if a staff member seems to falling behind the standard of the office, the data can pinpoint where they may need coaching. KPIs can show if the staff member needs coaching in capture rate, premium lens sales, or annual supply sales.

Once you have a KPI dashboard software, you then need to understand the story that the data is telling you. While at times the narrative may seem obvious, there are times when it is less obvious. Let's look at some examples:

Total Revenue is Down

When this is the case, there are three primary categories to begin investigating: Number of exams, Capture rate, and the total revenue per exam.

1. Number of Exams is down: review the schedule, exam recall methods, and the provider schedules to ensure maximization of the schedule.
2. Capture Rate is down: This one is a bit more tricky. This could be a staff training issue, a pricing issue, or a change in insurance plans or competition.
3. Revenue per exam is down: This could have multiple contributing factors from the types of products which are sold, the types of insurance patients have, and the types of disease states. Further, each of the areas affecting the capture rate will also affect revenue per exam. Consider which types of insurance may have saturated the schedule and whether they are profitable plans.

Contact Lens Revenue is Down

In this case, begin to look at several key metrics: Annual supply sales, daily wear lens sales, and total contact lens sales/fittings. There are key questions to ask:

1. Is the staff well versed in selling annual supplies?
2. Does the staff sell contacts along with eyewear sales?
3. Do all providers offer contact lens options when appropriate?

4. Are providers fitting as many daily wear, multifocal, and toric lenses as average?
5. Is it simple and convenient to re-order lenses through our office?
6. Are my patients ordering online?

Because KPI software aggregates and synthesizes data, it is important to remember that the reports may not always exactly match reports within your PMS system. Another reason that reports may not match is related to the data entry habits of your staff. Better input equals better output. Often times staff may not be able to find a new lens in the system and may manually enter a new lens or simply sell it under the name of an old lens. This type of practice can greatly skew your data over time. It is paramount that new products are regularly and properly entered into the product list of the PMS system. This allows the KPI software to accurately map products to the appropriate report lines.

Fitting Specialty Eyewear

Learning to fit eyewear for specific tasks is not only beneficial to the patient, but it can also position the dispenser as an eyewear expert. Your staff's ability to design and fit custom lens options can greatly enhance your credibility and patient loyalty.

Fitting specialty eyewear requires a basic understanding of prescription types with the staff. The following is a very basic guide for staff to understand prescriptions and specialty eyewear:

Multifocal lenses are designed to correct vision at multiple distances, accommodating the needs of individuals with presbyopia and other vision issues. These lenses typically feature multiple zones, each tailored for different viewing distances: near, intermediate, and far. The near vision zone is optimized for activities like reading and smartphone use, the intermediate zone is intended for tasks such as computer work and viewing objects at arm's length, and the distance zone is crafted for seeing clearly at greater distances, such as driving or watching TV. The design and layout of these zones can vary depending on the specific type of multifocal lens, such as bifocals, trifocals, or progressive lenses. Progressive lenses, for instance, offer a gradual transition between zones without the visible lines found in bifocals and trifocals, providing a more seamless and aesthetically pleasing solution.

Multifocal lenses, while offering the convenience of addressing multiple vision needs in one lens, come with specific limitations depending on the type: bifocals, trifocals, and progressive lenses. Each type has its unique challenges for certain tasks:

Bifocals

Bifocal lenses are divided into two distinct sections: the upper part for distance vision and the lower part for near vision.

Limitations:

1. Intermediate Vision Tasks:

Bifocals lack an intermediate vision zone, making tasks like computer work or viewing objects at arm's length uncomfortable. Users may find themselves constantly tilting their heads to find a clear view.

2. Image Jump:

The abrupt change between the two viewing zones can cause an "image jump" when moving the eyes from the distance to the near zone, which can be disorienting.

3. Aesthetic Concerns:

The visible line separating the two zones can be cosmetically unappealing to some users.

4. Temporary usability:

Patients who are fit with a lined bifocal will soon need intermediate accommodation. Since the bifocal offers only near (about 16 inches) and infinity (at the top), the patient will eventually complain that their bifocal no longer helps them. These scenarios are often overlooked in dispensing as the patient ages. The optometrist adjusts the add power and often assumes that the optician will inform them if the patient needs to convert to a trifocal or progressive while the optician assumes that the optometrist will inform the patient of the potential design change. The common result is that the patient returns shortly after receiving their new bifocal complaining that they cannot see intermediate distance objects.

Trifocals

Description: Trifocal lenses include three distinct sections: the top for distance vision, a middle section for intermediate vision, and the bottom for near vision.

Limitations:

1. Segmental Discomfort:

The presence of three distinct zones can lead to discomfort or difficulty in adjusting the eyes, especially for tasks requiring quick refocusing between distances.

2. Narrow Intermediate Zone:

The intermediate zone in trifocals can be narrow, limiting its effectiveness for extended computer use or other intermediate tasks. The overall height of the common trifocal design is only 7-8 millimeters. This may be challenging for some tasks. This also may require a lot of head tilt in order to achieve the proper zone.

3. Visible Lines:

Similar to bifocals, trifocals have visible lines separating the zones, which can be distracting and cosmetically unappealing.

Progressive Lenses

Description: Progressive lenses provide a smooth, gradual transition between multiple focal points (distance, intermediate, and near), with no visible lines. The benefit of these lenses is a "one size fits all" approach where the user is able to see at each distance. But I often explain to users that just as an SUV may be a multi-purpose vehicle, it isn't necessarily good for the racetrack or for hauling dirt. A person's lifestyle may necessitate additional pairs of eyewear.

Limitations:

    1.   Peripheral Distortion:

The lens design can cause peripheral distortion or "swim effect," where the edges of the visual field appear blurry or distorted, which can be particularly troublesome for activities requiring peripheral awareness, such as driving.

    2.   Adaptation Period:

Users often require an adaptation period to get used to the smooth transition between zones. Initial discomfort and dizziness are common.

    3.   Limited Intermediate Width:

Despite the seamless transition, the intermediate zone can still be relatively narrow, posing challenges for tasks like computer work where a wider field of intermediate vision is beneficial. For modern computer users with multiple screens, this can be a considerable challenge. For new progressive wearers, I often ask them how many computer screens they typically use when working. They also require head tilt in order to utilize the intermediate an near zones which may be uncomfortable for extended periods.

4. Cost:

Progressive lenses tend to be more expensive than bifocals and trifocals due to their complex design and the absence of visible lines.

General Limitations Across All Multifocal Lenses

5. Reading Small Print:

Multifocal lenses might not be as effective for prolonged reading of very small print, requiring users to use additional magnifying tools or separate reading glasses.

6. Specific Task Optimization:

No single lens type can be perfectly optimized for all tasks, meaning that users might still face challenges with specific activities, such as extended computer use, detailed craftwork, or sports.

7. Custom Fit:

Proper fitting and customization by an experienced optometrist are crucial. Poor fitting can exacerbate the limitations and discomfort associated with multifocal lenses.

By understanding these limitations, users can make more informed decisions and possibly consider having different types of glasses for different activities, ensuring the best possible vision correction for their lifestyle.

Single vision eyewear is designed to correct vision for a specific distance, offering several benefits for distance, computer, and close activities. Here's a detailed look at the advantages for each type of activity:

Distance Vision

Description: Single vision lenses for distance are typically prescribed to correct nearsightedness (myopia) or farsightedness (hyperopia).

Benefits:

1.   Wide Field of Clear Vision:

These lenses provide a broad, uninterrupted field of vision for distant objects, making them ideal for activities like driving, watching TV, or outdoor sports.

2.   Reduced Eye Strain:

They minimize the effort required to focus on distant objects, reducing eye strain and fatigue.

3.   Optimal Peripheral Vision:

Single vision lenses do not have the peripheral distortions often associated with multifocal lenses, providing clearer side vision.

4.   Cost-Effective:

Typically less expensive than multifocal lenses, making them a budget-friendly option for those primarily needing correction for a specific task such as sewing, computer use, reading, or driving.

Computer Use (Intermediate Vision)

Description: Single vision lenses for computer use are tailored to correct vision at the typical distance between the user and the computer screen, generally considered an intermediate range.

Benefits:

1. Enhanced Comfort:

Designed specifically for the intermediate range, these lenses reduce eye strain and discomfort associated with prolonged computer use.

2. Improved Posture:

Users do not need to tilt their heads or adjust their posture to find a clear focus, promoting better ergonomics.

3. Wide Field of View:

These lenses offer a clear, wide field of vision at the intermediate distance, making it easier to view multiple monitors or large screens. The patient is then able to glance around the screens without needing to move their head to stay in the clear zone of the progressive.

4. Blue Light Protection:

Many single-vision lenses are available in the market with embedded blue light protection in a stock single-vision lens. This can be a cost-effective option for the patient while increasing margins for the office.

Close Activities (Near Vision)

Description: Single-vision lenses for near vision are typically prescribed for tasks requiring close focus, such as reading, sewing, or detailed work.

Benefits:

1. Precise Focus:

These lenses provide sharp, clear vision for close-up tasks, enhancing the ability to see fine details.

2. Reduced Eye Fatigue:

By offering a tailored solution for near vision, these lenses help reduce eye fatigue and strain associated with prolonged reading or detailed work. This is an important option for patients with complex eye pathology which may limit their visual acuity across the visual field.

3. Customizable:

Near vision lenses can be customized with additional features like anti-reflective coatings, further enhancing comfort and clarity during close-up tasks.

General Benefits of Single Vision Eyewear

1. Simplicity:

Single vision lenses offer a straightforward solution for specific vision needs, eliminating the complexity of adjusting to multiple focal points.

2. Adaptation:

Users typically find it easier to adapt to single vision lenses compared to multifocal lenses, as there are no transitions between different vision zones.

3. Cost:

Generally, more affordable than multifocal lenses, single vision lenses are a cost-effective option for individuals needing correction at one specific distance.

4. Aesthetic Appeal:

Single vision lenses often have a thinner profile compared to multifocal lenses, making them more aesthetically pleasing.

Conclusion

Single vision eyewear, tailored to correct vision at a specific distance, provides targeted benefits for distance, computer, and close activities. They offer clear, comfortable vision without the complexities and potential distortions of multifocal lenses. While they may require switching between different pairs of glasses for different tasks, their specialized focus can greatly enhance visual clarity and comfort for specific activities.

Calculating the prescription for single vision readers from a bifocal prescription involves focusing on the "add" value in the bifocal prescription, which indicates the additional correction needed for near vision. Before performing any calculations, be sure to review your state and local laws regarding what is allowable by a licensed optician in your area. Laws regarding what must be done by the refracting physician and the optometrist may vary by jurisdiction. Here's a step-by-step guide on how to do the calculation for reading:

Step-by-Step Calculation

1. **Understand the Bifocal Prescription:**

   o A typical bifocal prescription includes values for distance vision and an "add" value for near vision. The format looks like this:

      ▪ OD (Right Eye): -2.00 (distance) +2.00 (add)

      ▪ OS (Left Eye): -1.50 (distance) +2.00 (add)

2. **Identify the Distance Prescription:**

   o The distance part of the prescription is used for seeing far away. In the example above:

      ▪ OD: -2.00

      ▪ OS: -1.50

3. **Identify the Add Value:**

   o The "add" value indicates the additional power needed for reading or close-up work. In this example:

      ▪ Add: +2.00 for both eyes

4. **Calculate the total Reading Prescription for single vision:**

   o Add the "add" value to the distance prescription to get the reading prescription.

- For OD: -2.00 (distance) + 2.00 (add) = 0.00

- For OS: -1.50 (distance) + 2.00 (add) = +0.50

Example Calculation

Given Bifocal Prescription:

- **OD (Right Eye)**: -2.00 (distance) +2.00 (add)

- **OS (Left Eye)**: -1.50 (distance) +2.00 (add)

Step-by-Step Calculation:

1. **Right Eye (OD):**

   o Distance: -2.00

   o Add: +2.00

   o Reading Prescription: -2.00 + 2.00 = 0.00 (Plano, or no additional power needed)

2. **Left Eye (OS):**

   o Distance: -1.50

   o Add: +2.00

   o Reading Prescription: -1.50 + 2.00 = +0.50

Resulting Single Vision Reading Prescription:

- **OD (Right Eye)**: Plano (0.00)

- **OS (Left Eye)**: +0.50

Additional Considerations

1. **Astigmatism Correction:**

   o If the bifocal prescription includes a cylindrical correction (for astigmatism), you need to include this in the reading prescription. The "add" value only affects the spherical component.

   o Example:

     ▪ OD: -2.00 - 0.50 x 180 + 2.00 (add)

     ▪ OS: -1.50 - 0.75 x 90 + 2.00 (add)

     ▪ Calculated reading prescription:

       ▪ OD: Plano (0.00) - 0.50 x 180

       ▪ OS: +0.50 - 0.75 x 90

2. **Check with an Optometrist:**

   o While the calculation is straightforward, it's always a good idea to have the final prescription verified by an optometrist to ensure accuracy and suitability for your needs.

Summary

To convert a bifocal prescription to single vision readers, simply add the "add" value to the distance prescription for each eye. Ensure you include any cylindrical correction if applicable, and consult with an optometrist for the best results.

Intermediate Power Calculations

To calculate the intermediate power, there are two common methods: ratio and dioptric demand. The ratio method involves multiplying the prescribed near add power by a ratio which is related to the working distance. Basically, the ratio assumes that 16 inches or 40cm the percentage of add power is 100% (Be sure to check with the optometrist to know that this was the distance chosen, patients may describe different near distances). The ratio then assumes that the patient needs about 50% of their add power at intermediate. This may vary by patient. The dioptric demand method is more scientific and uses a formula to calculate the demand needed for each distance of focus.

Ratio Method for calculating intermediate power.

Calculating the intermediate prescription from a multifocal (bifocal or progressive) prescription involves adjusting the prescription to focus on intermediate distances, typically around 20-30 inches, which is useful for tasks like computer work. This calculation typically involves using half of the "add" value provided in the multifocal prescription. However, the patient's needs may vary based upon distance. For the best result using the ratio method, I recommend the following method of determining the midrange power:

> 1. Using a trial frame, mockup the full prescription (distance plus the add power) in three options 40% of the add

power, 50% of the add power, and 60% of the add power.

2. Then have the patient hold a reading card at the distance in which they will be using the task specific eyewear. For a computer screen, I will often have them sit at a desk to view a screen or hold the reading card for them.

3. Then I will have them try each pair and record which one works the best for them.

Here's a detailed guide on how to perform this calculation:

Step-by-Step Calculation

1. **Understand the Multifocal Prescription:**

   o A typical multifocal prescription includes values for distance vision and an "add" value for near vision. The format looks like this:

      ▪ OD (Right Eye): -2.00 (distance) +2.00 (add)

      ▪ OS (Left Eye): -1.50 (distance) +2.00 (add)

2. **Identify the Distance Prescription:**

   o The distance part of the prescription is used for seeing far away. In the example above:

- OD: -2.00

- OS: -1.50

3. **Identify the Add Value:**

   o The "add" value indicates the additional power needed for near vision. In this example:

     - Add: +2.00 for both eyes

4. **If using 50% of the add power, calculate half of the Add Value:**

   o To determine the intermediate prescription, you typically use half of the "add" value.

     - Add: +2.00

     - Half of Add: +2.00 / 2 = +1.00

5. **Calculate the Intermediate Prescription:**

   o Add the half of the "add" value to the distance prescription to get the intermediate prescription.

     - For OD: -2.00 (distance) + 1.00 (half of add) = -1.00

     - For OS: -1.50 (distance) + 1.00 (half of add) = -0.50

Example Calculation

Given Multifocal Prescription:

- **OD (Right Eye)**: -2.00 (distance) +2.00 (add)

- **OS (Left Eye)**: -1.50 (distance) +2.00 (add)

Step-by-Step Calculation:

1. **Right Eye (OD):**

   - Distance: -2.00

   - Add: +2.00

   - Half of Add: +1.00

   - Intermediate Prescription: -2.00 + 1.00 = -1.00

2. **Left Eye (OS):**

   - Distance: -1.50

   - Add: +2.00

   - Half of Add: +1.00

   - Intermediate Prescription: -1.50 + 1.00 = -0.50

Resulting Intermediate Prescription:

- **OD (Right Eye)**: -1.00

- **OS (Left Eye)**: -0.50

Summary

To convert a multifocal prescription to an intermediate prescription, you add half of the "add" value to the distance prescription for each eye. Be sure to include any cylindrical correction if applicable and consult with an optometrist for verification. This intermediate prescription is particularly useful for tasks that require focus at an intermediate distance, such as computer work or other activities at arm's length.

The Dioptric Demand Method for calculating intermediate add power:

This method involves using a formula to calculate the dioptric demand at each distance. In order to understand dioptric demand, we will look at the accommodative ability for each age group and the formula for demand.

Adjusting for Specific Distances

The "add" power is also influenced by the specific distance at which the near tasks are performed. Here's a step-by-step method to adjust the "add" power for different working distances using the formula for dioptric demand:

1. **Determine the Near Working Distance:**

    o Standard near working distance is typically around 40 cm (16 inches). This distance requires +2.50 of "demand power". Demand power is the amount of accommodation that they eyes need in order to focus at this distance. This is not the same as their add power. Their add power is a reflection of how much natural accommodation they have lost due to age. The add power is prescribed to help the patient reach the total demand power.

    o For computer work or other intermediate tasks, the distance might be around 50-

75 cm (20-30 inches). If the patient seems unsure of their working distance, I may ask them to measure at their own desk or work station.

2. **Use the Diopter Formula:** It is assumed that an average patient needs +2.50 diopters of demand power in order to read at 16 inches or about 60cm. As we age, we lose this accommodative ability of this demand power. For example, a patient who is prescribed an add power of +1.50 is assumed to have about +1.00 of accommodation remaining for demand power. As the person ages, they lose this accommodation even more. This loss increases the need for accurate calculations of distance-specific prescriptions. The less remaining accommodation that the patient has, the more they will need help with each specific distance. This is why some patients may be fine with a lined bifocal at first, but in the following years may complain that objects at arm's length are also blurry. The demand power formula assumes that the total demand for 16 inches is +2.50.

- o **D=1/f** In this formula, you will determine the standard power demand or dioptric demand for reading at a particular distance. The "f" will be the distance in meters. For example, a patient who uses an intermediate at a distance of 60 centimeters would input an "f" value of .60m. In this case, the power demand at this distance is 1.67.

60 centimeters = .60 meters, So the formula would populate as below:

D=1/.60

Then **D=1.67**

- ○ **Calculate the difference in demand power:** The standard demand is 2.50 diopters at 40cm. This is important because the doctor will typically prescribe the add power (often based on age) to this distance of 40cm or about 16 inches. In order to calculate the difference in the demand power, subtract the result of the above formula from the standard of +2.50 total accommodation.

+2.50-1.67=.83   (.83 is the difference in demand power)

At the distance used above of 60cm, this difference is .83. This means that in order to find the power for the distance of 60cm, we must subtract this amount from the total add power which is prescribed to this patient.

- ○ **Calculate the Resulting Intermediate add power:** For this calculation, simply take the prescribed near add power.

Near Add Power – Difference in Demand Power = Intermediate Add Power

Example Calculation

Let's calculate the "add" power for a person in their mid-40s who needs glasses for computer work at an intermediate distance of 60 cm.

1. **Age-Based Add Power:**

   o Mid-40s typically require +1.00 to +1.50 D for standard near tasks at 40 cm. For this example, we will assume that the doctor prescribed a +1.50 for the add power at 16 inches or about 40 cm.

2. **Adjust for Intermediate Distance:**

   o The power needed for 60 cm is 1.67 based on the formula **D=1/f** where "f" is the focal length of 60 cm or .60m

   o Since the age-based add power for 40 cm has been prescribed for this patient at 1.50, we will continue calculations for adjustment based upon this.

Steps to Adjust

1. **Determine the Diopter Difference:**

   o Near task at 40 cm requires +2.50 D (standard).

   o Intermediate task at 60 cm requires +1.67 D.

   o Difference: +2.50 - +1.67 = +0.83 D.

2. **Adjust the Add Power for this distance:**

   o If the prescribed add power is +1.50 D for 40 cm, then for 60 cm:

- o Prescribed Add Power - Difference = Adjusted Add Power.

- o Example: +1.50 - +0.83 = +0.67 D (This can be rounded to +0.75 D).

3. **Use the resulting Add Power to the distance rx to create single vision intermediate lenses for this distance**

- o Add +.75 to the distance prescription

Now that you understand the calculations, there are many custom pairs of eyewear that you can make for nearly any task. Musicians, speakers, and hobbyists may all have very specific distances that they need to work at. Understanding the exact distance where they work is the first step. This process begins by uncovering the patient's lifestyle, interests, and hobbies to ensure that you are fitting them with eyewear that will fully benefit them.

Once you have mastered fitting custom single vision eyewear, there are many other options which could also serve your patients in their hobby or daily work. For example, an older person who has lost most of their accommodative ability could also benefit from adding their remaining add power to the bottom segment of a multifocal for their computer or hobby eyewear.

- o If the patient had a prescribed add power of +2.50, and an adjusted intermediate power of +1.50, then this patient has a remaining add power of +1.00 which could be added to the bottom to aid in tasks at 40 cm or 16 inches.

Computer Progressives

Just as you could put near at the bottom of a lined bifocal and intermediate at the top, you could also create something similar in a no-line design. These are often called computer lenses or office lenses. They come in multiple designs to match the needs of your patient.

They can have near at the bottom and computer at the top, near at the bottom and room-distance at the top, or computer at the bottom and room-distance at the top.

Since these lenses do not progress the full spectrum from near to infinity, the designs are able to accomplish a much wider channel through the progression with less peripheral blur.

Most lens manufacturers offer varying designs of computer progressives with many similarities in designs. These manufacturers each offer different computer lens designs within their portfolio.

To fit a computer progressive, first determine the most important distances that the patient needs. Next, select a lens design that offers these distances. Finally, fit the lens in a similar manner to measuring a progressive.

Single Vision Boost Lenses

Single vision boost lenses are designed to relieve eye strain at near focus. The demands of today's digital devices can cause eye strain for all ages. These lens designs incorporate the benefits of a single vision lens with a minor dynamic add power at the bottom.

The dynamic ranges for the designs span from about +50 up to +1.32. These are beneficial to digital device users as young as adolescents and strong enough for early presbyopic patients.

Using the skills you have learned combined with technology from lens designers, you can become a trusted source of custom eyewear to your patients. You can now serve them with golf glasses, spa glasses, computer glasses, or gaming glasses. The possibilities are endless!